# Equality

## Promotes Blind Justice

Reverend Willie Pou

authorHOUSE®

*AuthorHouse™*
*1663 Liberty Drive, Suite 200*
*Bloomington, IN 47403*
*www.authorhouse.com*
*Phone: 1-800-839-8640*

*First published by AuthorHouse 12/29/2008*

*ISBN: 978-1-4389-3562-1 (sc)*

*Printed in the United States of America*
*Bloomington, Indiana*

*This book is printed on acid-free paper.*

# Contents

# Dedication

I dedicate this book to my children, Lavetta Brumfield, Paxton James Pou, Willie Pou, Jr., and my Grandchildren. Further, I dedicate this story to my four sisters, Ennie Mae Warren, Elouise Richey, Dorinda Pou-Gray and Girtha Pou; one living in Las Vegas, one in Dallas, Texas and two in Mississippi; plus lots of other relatives in Las Vegas and nearby Los Angeles, California.

All of whom helped guide my footsteps. Two of my sisters actually sent my plane fair for travel to Las Vegas; which is why I decided on Las Vegas knowing that Los Angeles was not far away.

Also, I would like to dedicate this book to Mr. Michael Vick. The glory to God I acknowledge; I believe no matter what you do, you should always put God first. Next I dedicate this book to those who have had their lives taken unjustly at the hands of those who go unpunished; and to those who suffer because of an unspoken legal discretionary right to discriminate within the justice system for no good reason which still exists.

# Acknowledgment

First, I give honor to *God* for ordering my steps. I confer special thanks to all that motivated me in my writing and documentation of this story which has gone so lightly on the hearts of some. Further, I am thankful for my children, nieces, nephews, sisters, aunties, and all my relatives, each and every one of you I thank you for being a part of my life.

Special thanks to my Editor/Coordinator and Story Analyst at BookPubCo: http://www.bookpubco.net.

# Preface

Reverend Willie Pou has observed many cases of social injustice in American society for many years, which he believes from a moral perspective, are unfair. There are two cases he is profoundly interested in at this time. In his words they are both deeply and morally troubling to him. He further believes; that they should be brought to the attention of other like-minded *Americans*. As for the moral issues surrounding these two cases that have aroused Reverend Pou's interest this time; the first case is about the medical doctor from New Orleans, Louisiana who used morphine to overdose four elderly patents, but was found not guilty by a jury of her peers.

The second case is about a young *African-American* who was a National Football League (NFL) superstar from Atlanta, Georgia who bet on dog fights and was found guilty by a single Judge, not of his peer group; and then sent to jail for inhumane treatment of dogs. It is a known fact that the doctor's actions ended the lives of four elderly patients under her care, during the storm of Hurricane Katrina through a process identified as euthanasia. However, in contrast the football player was accused of destroying dogs that were injured after the dogs lost a dog fight.

The justice system in these two cases appears to have used a legal discretionary right to discriminate against the one who was charged with what appears to be the lesser crime. The courts demonstrated this unspoken discretion in these two cases and in separate municipalities and courts with different Judges. The medical doctor in the Louisiana case was adjudicated in a Louisiana courtroom and not indicted for allegedly having overdosed four patients on morphine; causing the deaths of all four. The NFL superstar on the other hand was accused of "cruel and inhumane" treatment towards dogs; for his crimes he was prosecuted and sentenced to prison for allowing his dogs to fight each other for profit.

This book is a fascinating read about the legal discretionary right to discriminate and how two similar situations coming before the legal system are processed completely differently. One dealing with the cruelty to human life, and another with the ill treatment of animals; where the legal system appears to place a higher value on the life of animals than the value of human life. The author highlights the differences in how the legal system allows the courts' judges to place different values on the punishment it levies for similar cases. The author has chosen these two very distinct cases to contrast the differences in how justice is applied in the legal system.

Reverend Pou desires you the reader to understand the background of each of the accused and their alleged crimes. He wants you to imagine that the NFL superstar was a <u>white male</u> member of the dominant culture within the highest status class and decide for yourself if the punishments fit the crimes.

The author sets the stage for a debate about morality and the integrity of the *American* justice system; a debate never before experienced out in the open where other morally concerned *Americans* can participate. The author tells about each character's crime and the events leading up to their misbehavior. He contrasts two lives and expresses his opinion about how unfair the justice system is for a member of a status cast group without society's automatic support for legal representation!

*Carrie Johnson*
Editor/Coordinator

# Chapter One
## Deeply Troubling Moral Issues

### Discretionary Right to Discriminate

This story involves a high profile *African-American* NFL superstar, who suffered at the discretion of the legal system, because of the inferior status conferred upon his group. Because of his status and regardless of his individual economic contribution to society he did not benefit from the inherent legal support afforded other members of society. Often it is *African-Americans* who are the beneficiaries of a discretionary discriminatory justice system's negative outcome, while members of the dominant culture with similar or less economic status are the beneficiary of positive outcomes. There are many stories throughout history that prove this hypothesis true!

The following high profile case helps to confirm this theory. On the morning of April 24, 2008, "the famous actor" Wesley Snipes after being indicted for 'Tax evasion' was convicted and sentenced (Source: CNN). This case emphasizes the "legal discretionary discriminatory" practice of the *American* justice system. A practice based on an exclusionary policy based value system, which is opposed to the *African-Americans'* desire for an inclusionary, or equality based value system. This practice started with the *Betrayal of 1877*, after the *blacks* won the civil war and the *whites* won the battle over reconstruction/affirmative action. Take the case of the famous actor, you might ask why not levy a fine of proportion to fit the crime as is the practice in many cases that deals

1

with white collar crimes, rather than a sentence. Why the justice system would chose to punish such a viable, active and productive member of our society with prison is questionable to say the least! A strong monetary fine would have sent a message to fit the crime.

This unfair and unequal justice was at its best when the *American* people were given "the unfair sentencing laws" that clearly drew a dividing line between the status groups. For example *African-American* youth receive longer sentences than due *white* youth for the same amount of cocaine. The case of Sean Bell is another case that boggles the mind when it comes to the immorality of injustice; this young *African-America*n was shot 51 times by officers of the New York Police Department one day before he was to be married. He was unarmed yet three police officers shot him 51 times and each officer was acquitted of all charges by a single Judge.

There were no jurors seated to hear the legal arguments. The Judge cited concerns about inciting too much emotional response to the perceived insensitive behavior of the police officers. Because of the imbalances in the legal system, the Judge was further allowed to find the three officers not guilty of any criminal action. The Judge was free to make this ruling based on a built-in discretionary discriminatory practice used by the *American* criminal justice system. Could it be assumed that because the victim is dead that he forfeited any rights to a jury trial or should there always be an asserted right for a jury for the dead? This exclusionary belief system is more widely used when it comes to *African-Americans who are* without any social recognizable right to automatic legal representation. This built-in discretion excludes even high profile *African-Americans* from any expectation of the *American ideal* of a fair and balanced justice system for all who share the same values. All these cases have brought to focus the imbalances in the justice system.

I am deeply interested in the case of the doctor whose case was reported back in 2005, after the Hurricane Katrina storm in New Orleans on, August 29, 2005. Because she made the choice to save herself, the patients under her care suffered their death. It was alleged she opted to overdose four elderly patients with morphine, effectively taking their lives so she could escape the flood. Because of her crime, she was arrested for murder, but found not guilty of any crimes. In contrasting still another case of which I am intensely interested in; the court's judge ruled that the NFL superstar should go to jail for his participation in raising dogs for the purpose of dog fighting. He later participated in euthanizing the dogs that were injured and lost the fight for the purpose of taking them out of their pain. Although these are separate and unique incidents, *Americans* focused on the dog fighting media frenzy, rather than the human euthanizing simply because of the celebrity status of the NFL superstar. These two cases caught my attention as well as many other *Americans* when he was convicted, but the doctor was not affected due to her status as a doctor of medicine. Although euthanizing humans should be a more serious moral crime. Thus the following question that we as *Americans* in our society should be asking is: "Are the lives of dogs more important than human life for the purpose punishment, regardless of who commits the crime?"

## The Hard Choice

The doctor continues to practice medicine even after it was determined that she killed four intensive-care patients during the Hurricane Katrina tragedy in New Orleans. According to sources all charges against the Louisiana doctor were dropped. The mitigating factors, no doubt supported the hard decision she had to make, either to save her-self from the flooding waters or stay with her patients that could not help themselves. The patients had been moved upward from floor to floor, but the water kept rising. The Doctor was left with <u>the hard choice</u>, to save herself and she decided to do just that. Rather than to leave the patients helpless to fend for themselves, she injected them with morphine, which allowed each of them to die peacefully.

Doctors are legally bound by an ethical oath of conduct to do no harm. The doctor has to have known the law, and taken the oath to do no harm, as all doctors do. So the doctor becomes the postal child that represents the imbalances in the justice system; therefore I leave this case in the hands of my *GOD*. I do not know what I myself would have done in the same situation. But it appears to be a striking injustice that she would not be found guilty, but the NFL superstar would be found guilty and put in prison for betting on dog fights.

With that being said, there are many cases that come to mind of a far lesser nature than killing human beings, one of which is that of the NFL superstar, Michael Vick, who was accused of breaking the law by betting on dog-fights. He was convicted for what appeared, to be a lesser crime, however he was put in prison after a rather brief trial, whereas the doctor got away with a more serious crime. This is where some judges appear to be playing *God* by using their legal discretion to discriminate against whomever they want; such is the case of "*God* Blesses whomever he wants".

Although, Michael has not been accused of killing anyone, he has been stripped of his wealthy life style and status, and thrown into prison. In comparing these two cases something seems terribly wrong with the fairness of *America's* justice system and how justice is dispensed. This unanswered question keeps coming to my mind of: Are the lives of animals more important than humans? According to the *Bible*, human life is superior to all other forms of life; for *He, God* made man in his own image and woman in the image of man. However, this principle did not work in favor of the NFL superstar as it did for the doctor in question.

## Tried - Convicted - Sentenced

The NFL superstar, arguably the greatest football quarterback ever to play was drafted by the National Football League (NFL) in 2001. He received more than $20 million dollars as a signing bonus with the Atlanta Falcons of which he may have to repay $3.75 million of it because of his conviction. It has been reported that he has received over $37 million in total from the Falcons. Part of my growing concern about this NFL superstar is how much will he lose in comparison to what the doctor has gained. It has been said and judged by many that he and some of his friends operated a rather lucrative and sophisticated dog fighting and gambling ring. Participants reportedly invested money to back up the NFL superstar's conclusions that a specific dog would win the fight. He was subsequently arrested, tried, convicted and sentenced to 23 months in prison, on Monday, December 10, 2007, for running a "cruel and inhumane" dog fighting ring and lying about it. Although there is no parole in the federal system; rules governing time off for good behavior could reduce his prison stay by approximate three months. This would result in his early release somewhere during the summer of 2009. He has been suspended without pay by the NFL and he has lost all his lucrative endorsement deals since his indictment in the summer of 2007. The doctor on the other hand, was never suspended from practicing medicine and continues to maintain her reputation as a "good doctor". The question keeps coming to my mind: Does society levy justice according to the crime?

Should not the punishment be more severe for a physician accused of inhumane treatment of their patients, than that of a football star running an enterprising dog-fighting ring? You shall see in the chapters that follow, that the punishment for taking human life was less severe than for taking an injured dog's life. Michael Vick received a greater punishment for his mistreatment of dogs than the Doctor for taking human lives. It is important to discuss the background of each of these individual cases in order to understand how the legal system supported by society, treats members of each status cast system differently; thereby making punishment for the crimes committed by persons from the assumed and asserted "lower-status class" group more dreadful than that of those of the "upper-status class".

Judges, jurors, and bystanders alike all bring their beliefs to our table of justice; beliefs which normally originate from their own backgrounds and experiences. These experiences include teachings about established rules of law and unspoken discretions that are allowed to influence rulings in the legal system along with their ability to use the practice against whoever they wish. I believe however that all of these players bring along their own jealousies, prejudices and bias, which includes socially, supported stereotypical views of one another. This is where *American's* society might very well benefit from; taking a long hard look at ways in which it might become a more united *group of* people as opposed to being a more divided group of people. Although *America* is now in the 21st century, she continues to discount the rights and wealth of those who are in the "lower-status class" of *America's* cast system. Wealth should improve the status of *African-Americans* in the eyes of society, but it does not. Applications of laws, which are hundreds of years old are continuously applied differently based on one's status-level. Much can be said about the unfairness of how the laws of this country are rendered in an attempt to continue to enforce a rule of law that allows justice to be administered differently based on one's status-level. Often times that *blind justice* mask is shifted to the side and feeds upon their own jealousies, prejudices and bias! The ways, in which today's progressive minded *Americans* view status-issues are not the same ways people viewed them in the past, dating as far back as 1877. Things may have appeared to have changed; but the court system continues to uphold historical views about status, opportunity and privilege.

## Historical Linked Biases

While researching these cases I found it increasing difficult to understand how the law could justify and excuse a doctor for placing such a low value on human life. I find it hard to believe that our justice system could even start to explain how it applied sentencing in the cases of the doctor and the NFL superstar. There is a dream I keep on dreaming that we as a people will get beyond our preconceived views of one another regardless of the differences of our backgrounds. Eliminating many of the effects of these prejudgments of the *past* may very well be impossible, but when prejudgments are discussed and brought to consciousness, change maybe possible through self awareness.

# Chapter Two

## Facts Surrounding the Louisiana Case

### The Doctor's Upbringing

The Doctor is the seventh of eleven children of Hispanic and Italian heritage. She was born and raised in New Orleans. Her father came to New Orleans from the Dominican Republic. Both her father and two of her uncle's were doctors. She decided to follow in their footsteps while she was an undergraduate at Louisiana State University. She attended medical school there eight years later. She did her medical residency fellowships in Memphis, Pittsburgh and Indiana. She taught for five years at the University of Texas Medical Branch in Galveston before returning to New Orleans in September 2004. Her resume lists dozens of papers, articles and presentations on diseases and surgeries of the throat.

The doctor is an ear, nose and throat specialist and a surgeon as well; and an associate professor in the Department of Otorhinolaryngology at the Louisiana State University (LSU), Health Sciences Center in New Orleans. She was accused of administering lethal painkilling injections to four elderly intensive-care patients at Memorial Medical Center where she worked in New Orleans three days after the landfall of Hurricane Katrina. A year after her arrest in July 2006, a grand jury opted not to indict her on second degree murder charges, thus clearing her of all criminal charges.

## The Accusations and the Investigation

The intensive-care patients whom the doctor was accused of killing were patients of a company called *Lifecare*. *Lifecare* ran an acute care facility for extremely ill patients; the doctor and other medical staff were caring for these patients as the doctor who was assigned to care for them did not arrive for work.

The investigation apparently began after a physician working at Memorial following the hurricane; made public charges that one or more health care workers allegedly, had been responsible for the death of patients. The physician told the news media that his conclusion was based on conversations with other health care workers. After learning that another doctor was about to kill patients, he boarded a boat and left the hospital. He explained his actions in terms of his opposition to the attending physician's alleged actions. The doctor in question and the nurses were accused of being principals to second-degree murder, in the deaths of four patients at Memorial Medical Center, three days after Hurricane Katrina hit. On Tuesday, July 18, 2006, the Louisiana Attorney General arrested the doctor along with two nurses. The three of them were accused of being an accessory or principal to second-degree murder in the deaths of four patients. The incident took place at Memorial Medical Center on September 1, 2005, in New Orleans, Louisiana. The affidavit states that the doctor and two nurses intentionally killed four patients by administering or causing to be administered lethal doses of morphine sulphate and/or midazolam '*Versed*', which is a sedative. According to sources, none of the patients' records had doctors' order for '*Versed*'.

The charge carries a mandatory life sentence. The case was turned over to the New Orleans prosecutor, who would decide whether to ask a grand jury to bring charges against the medical professionals.

According to the head of the department at Louisiana State University and several other doctors the morphine and '*Versed*' that investigators found in the patients' bodies are commonly given to relieve a patient's suffering and anxiety.

## Social Support versus Opposition

Although the doctor had committed the worst kind of crime, her character was not harmed by her unprofessional behavior. The director of critical care at Charity Hospital said that he and others were angry about the accusations against the doctor and nurses who risked their own safety to provide care in a chaotic and frightening situation. He believes that the doctor and nurses were heroes. They stayed behind on their own to care for desperately ill people; although they had an opportunity to leave; they chose instead to stay and care for the patients. Attorneys for the trio say they are innocent. Another doctor said he believes this will likely make doctors who have left town less eager to return, as the city tries to recover from the hurricane. Some fear that in the future other health care providers might not want to help out by volunteering their services and putting their lives on the line. An intensive care emergency room doctor who himself stayed at Charity Hospital during Hurricane Katrina, said he believed that it could quite possibly even prevent health care providers from helping out at all in the future.

A spokeswoman for the Attorney General's office said her agency was investigating the claims at Memorial in order to enforce the law. The doctor and her associates were the first medical professionals charged during the months' long criminal investigation into whether many of New Orleans' sick and elderly were abandoned or put to death.

## Deplorable Conditions

It is true that the conditions under which the doctor and her associates worked were deplorable, as it was for many others. There were hundreds of people stranded in the hospitals with no power to run lights or elevators and no running water. There was no communication from floor to floor, much less to the outside world. The town was surrounded by water. After the storm hit the temperature was enormously intense; during normal conditions the city's temperature on a hot summer's day can literally take your breath away. Anyone who was willing to carry a gun was deputized to watch the entrances as people broke into nearby buildings. I can imagine that the people in the hospital suffered greatly, especially those who were unable to walk under such conditions, even patients who might have been able to walk and were relatively stable before Katrina could easily have lapsed into some sort of critical condition. Even relatively healthy people must have suffered from various types of illnesses during such a disastrous incident as Hurricane Katrina.

## Conditions at Memorial Medical

According to reports the conditions at Memorial were difficult following the hurricane.

When Hurricane Katrina hit in August 2005, the doctor and others were working at Memorial Medical Center even as the flood waters engulfed the hospital and filled its lower level. The hospital's ground floor and surrounding streets were flooded and the area was inundated by 10 feet of floodwater. Patients were threatened by not only their existing critical illness, but also suffocating heat and dehydration.

The 317 bed hospital had no electricity and the temperature inside rose as the staff tried to attend to patients while waiting four days to be evacuated. Without backup electrical power, temperatures reached 110 degrees, and at least 34 patients died, including some critically ill patients. Doctors could hear gunshots in the vicinity of the hospital, but despite the danger to their patients' they were told by officials, that evacuating Memorial was not as high a priority as evacuating citizens stranded on rooftops. More than 30 people died at Memorial; many from dehydration, during the four days before rescuers were able to get to the hospital. The people of New Orleans suffered a tremendous injustice due to the fact that our national emergency system was not equipped to handle such a disastrous situation.

## Deaths Undetermined

Autopsies were completed on the four patients connected to the only criminal case arising from hospital deaths during the chaotic days after Hurricane Katrina in New Orleans, Louisiana. The medical results were turned over to the district attorney's office as material evidence to be considered by a grand jury. The four patients were among a total of 34 who died at Memorial Hospital after Hurricane Katrina hit in 2005, and were the only ones that the Louisiana Attorney General's office found to be homicides. The Doctor and Nurses were arrested in the summer 2006, but they were never formally charged and were eventually set free on bond.

In February 2007, seven months after the doctor's initial arrest, the case against her and the two nurses appeared more questionable after Doctor Frank Minyard the Orleans Parish Coroner announced that he had classified the patient's deaths at Memorial as "undetermined," which meant that based on available evidence, he could not classify the deaths as being due to homicide or natural causes. Doctor Minyard reportedly told the local media that he had retained some of the nation's leading experts as consultants in the case. In mid-February 2007, the district attorney office's proceeded with their plans to impanel a grand jury to investigate the deaths at Memorial Medical Center. According to a representative from the district attorney's office rather than use the grand jury in a perfunctory manner, which is usually the modern practice, they planned to use the grand jury as an active investigative tool and subpoena witnesses. The district attorney declined to provide information on the grand jury's schedule or how long it expected the investigations to take.

The grand jury was finally sworn in on 6 March 2007, and the prosecutors took a rather unusual step by having their meetings at an undisclosed location; away from the courthouse in order to prevent the media from observing the identity of the witnesses coming and going. According to an assistant district attorney the grand jury would stay in place for one full year. It was selected to deal solely with the issues pertaining to the Memorial Medical Center's cases that developed as a result of Hurricane Katrina, rather than the hundreds grand juries cases normally heard; and prosecutors stated it could hear testimony for several months. These unusual moves prompted legal observers to speculate that the district attorney considered the evidence ambiguous and wanted to be able to assure the public of a thorough investigation if he decided to drop the case without bringing formal charges. These actions appeared suspicious, as though the actions being taken against the doctor were just for public show. After further review of the information regarding the autopsies and the various actions taken by the district attorney it became rather obvious that the scenario being set in place would do a grave injustice to the four victims. A Loyola University Law Professor told the media, "Doing it this way certainly speaks to the ambiguity of the evidence and the prosecutor's deliberation as to whether to seek an indictment. . . . Or it could be that he's made up his mind that he does not want to bring charges and wants the grand jury to provide his cover." The Grand Jury proceedings took several months to complete. Near the end of March 2007, the doctor's attorney told the media that a decision on the indictments could take until the end of April as both sides were involved in extensive investigations.

Initially, the New Orleans Parish Coroner was reported to have said, that after the toxicology test results came in he would be able to classify the deaths of the four patients; but until then he was unable to determine the causes of death. According to the coroner, the autopsies conducted on the four patients, like all the other autopsies which resulted from the hurricane; would be limited in scope as the autopsies had not been started until three weeks after the hurricane. So by the time the bodies were autopsied, they were actually severely decomposed.

The Attorney General said that he believed the women gave these desperately ill, stranded patients lethal injections of drugs after determining that the patients were either too ill or too incapacitated to be moved following Katrina. As far as he was concerned the doctor and the two nurses were murderers. But many in the medical community were outraged at the arrests, saying they believed the three caregivers were heroes who faced unimaginable horrors as Hurricane Katrina flooded the city and trapped them and their patients at Memorial. The women backed by the support of many medical professionals; denied any wrong-doing.

# Chapter Three

## The Facts Surrounding the Georgia Case

### The NFL Superstar's Upbringing

The NFL superstar was born June 26, 1980, in Newport News, Virginia. He was the second of four children. The other children were his older sister and younger siblings all born in Newport News, Virginia, who were raised by their two teenagers parents. His mother worked two jobs, obtained public assistance, and received help from her parents, while his father worked long hours in the shipyards as a sandblaster and spray-painter. They eventually married when the NFL superstar was about five years old; however, the children elected to continue using their father's surname, Vick. The family lived in "Ridley Circle Homes", a public housing project in a financially depressed and crime-ridden neighborhood located in the east end section of the port city. An area known in hip-hop culture by the slang names "Bad Newz" or "Bad News" according to the urban slang dictionary. The area the NFL superstar grew up in did not afford him the best environment to grow from. The area has not changed much from the years in which he lived there; by observations of the local people almost ten years after he left. There is drug dealing, drive-by shootings and constant killings in the neighborhood, and many have suggested that sports were a way out and a dream for many of the young youth in the area. The NFL superstar made it, but lacked some of the fundamental training and mentoring necessary to keep things straight.

During an interview in 2001, Michael told a news reporter at the Newport News *Daily Press* that when he was 10 or 11, he would go fishing even if the fish were not biting, just to get out of there and away from the violence and stress of daily life in the projects. The area in which he lived by all accounts was a troubled and complex environment for children to form a natural nurturing upbringing of a youthful heart. Many would find it hard to believe that dog fighting was a local activity there or in any environment that would care and nurture young children.

## Early Amateur Athletics

As a child, the NFL superstar went by the nickname "Ookie". During the early years of his family life, his father's employment required a lot of travel. But whenever he was home, he taught the fundamentals of football skills to his two sons. Also, Michael learned a lot about football from his second cousin; they both spent a lot of time as youths at the local Boys and Girls Club. As a 7-year-old throwing three touchdown passes in a Boys Club league, his apparent football talents led his coach and parents to keep special watch over his.

The NFL superstar told *Sporting News* magazine in an interview published April 9, 2001: "Sports kept me off the streets.... It kept me from getting into what was going on, the bad stuff. Lots of guys I knew have had bad problems."

## High School Years

The NFL superstar first came to prominence while at Homer L. Ferguson High School in Newport News, Virginia. As a freshman, he impressed many with his athletic ability by throwing the football over 400 yards during a game that year. After Ferguson High School closed in 1996 as part of a school modernization program for Newport News Public Schools; as a junior he and his Coach both moved to Warwick High, also in Newport News. During this time at Warwick High under the same Coach the superstar perfected his quarterback skills as a football player.

His Coach who also helped to guide his cousin from Newport News to the University of Virginia earlier; helped to assist the superstar and his family in choosing between Syracuse University in Syracuse, New York and Virginia Polytechnic Institute and the State University Virginia Tech in Blacksburg, Virginia. The Coach favored Virginia Tech where he felt the young superstar would receive better guidance under a Coach who promised to redshirt him and provide the freshman the needed time to develop. The young superstar was sold on the school's proximity to family and friends and apparently following his coach's advice, chose to attend Virginia Tech and play football as a Hokie.

He left the Newport News public housing projects in 1998, on the wings of *God's* glory on a college football scholarship. He was seen in the Newport News and the close by Hampton community of the lower Virginia Peninsula as a success story. In a story published in September 2000, while the NFL superstar was at Virginia Tech, his father told the University's *Collegiate Times*: "Ever since his son learned to throw a football, he's always liked throwing a ball.... It's just in his blood." He said that his son had never gotten into trouble or ... involved with drugs, adding: "I like the way he has developed, not only as a player but as a person". After becoming a standout high school football player in Virginia, he was awarded a scholarship to attend Virginia Tech, where his football career included a trip to the 2000 Sugar Bowl, the Bowl Championship Series title game.

## College Career

While attending Virginia Tech, after high school during his first collegiate game as a redshirt freshman against James Madison in 1999 the NFL superstar scored three rushing touchdowns in just over one quarter of play. His last touchdown was a spectacular flip, in which he landed awkwardly on his ankle, forcing him to miss the remainder of the game; in addition to the following game. During the season he successfully ran a last-minute game-winning drive against West Virginia in the annual Black Diamond Trophy rivalry game. He led the Hokies to an 11-0 season, straight to the Bowl Championship Series' national title game in the 2000 and later to the Nokia Sugar Bowl against Florida State. Although Virginia Tech lost 46-29, the NFL superstar was able to bring the team back from a 21 point deficit to take a brief lead. During the season he appeared on the cover of an ESPN sports magazine issue.

He was the forerunner of the National Collegiate Athletic Association in passing efficiency that year, setting a record as a freshman 180.4. Also, this was good enough for him to reach the third-highest all-time mark in comparison to another player that had set 185.9 from the 2006 season, at Hawaii. The NFL superstar was awarded an Excellence in Sports Performance Yearly (ESPY) Award as the nation's top college player. Further, he received the first-ever Archie Griffin Award as college football's most valuable player. In 1999, he was invited to the Heisman Trophy presentation and finished third in the voting. His third-place finish matched the highest finish ever by a freshman up to that point, the first being set by another superstar in 1980.

During the 2000 season, the NFL superstar had his share of highlights, such as his career rushing high of 210 yards against the Boston College Eagles in Chestnut Hill, Massachusetts. Then again in West Virginia in the Black Diamond Trophy game, the NFL superstar contributed two touchdowns and 288 total yards of offense to a 48-20 win. The following week, he led the Hokies back from a 14-0 deficit against Syracuse at the Carrier Dome a 50,000-seat sports' stadium located on Syracuse University Hill in New York, where the Hokies had not won since 1986. He stole the game with a 55-yard run with a minute thirty-four seconds left in the game.

Vick, the NFL superstar was injured in the following game against Pittsburgh and had to miss the rest of that game; the entire game against Central Florida and was unable to start against the Miami Hurricanes; the Hokies' loss of the season. The NFL superstar's final game at Virginia Tech came against the Clemson Tigers in the Toyota Gator Bowl where he was named *most valued player* of the game.

After his redshirt sophomore season, he was offered the opportunity and huge financial benefits as an option to leave Virginia Tech to become a professional football player. Aware that the rest of his family was still living in their 3 bedroom apartment in the Ridley Circle Homes; he was determined to buy his mother a home and car, therefore, he elected to leave Virginia Tech without graduating after three years to become the top 2001 NFL draft pick.

## Early Professional Career

In 2001 the NFL superstar was selected as the first overall drafts pick and first *African-American* quarterback chosen as number one in the NFL Draft. The San Diego Chargers had the number one selection spot in the draft that year, but traded the rights of the first overall choice to the Atlanta Falcons a day before the draft. Although Vick has never become league MVP, he finished second in voting in 2004. The NFL superstar made his NFL debut in San Francisco on September 9, 2001. He completed his first NFL pass with an 18-yard strike to his wide-receiver in the second quarter against Carolina on September 23rd; and his first NFL touchdown on a two-yard rushing score in the fourth quarter to help the Falcons to a 24-16 victory. He made his career start at Dallas on November 11th, by throwing the first touchdown pass of his career on a nine-yard toss to the tight-end in a 20-13 victory. In the two games, of which he started and of the eight games played that season, he completed 50 of 113 passes for 785 yards with two touchdowns and three interceptions; accounting for 234 of the team's 255 yards by the season finale in St. Louis on January 6, 2002. Further, he rushed 29 times for 289 yards, a 9.9 average with one touchdown.

By 2002, the NFL superstar had become a bona-fide star and MVP candidate all within his first season as a full time starter at the age of 22. He was named to his first Pro Bowl after starting in all 15 games played; only missing one game with the New York Giants on October 13, due to a sprained shoulder. He completed 231 of 421 passes for 2,936 yards and 16 touchdowns; both career-highs; he tallied 113 carries for 777 yards and eight rushing touchdowns. During that season, the NFL superstar established numerous single-game career-highs, including 24 passes completed and 46 pass attempts at Pittsburgh on November 10; as well as 337 passing yards against Detroit on December 22nd. The NFL superstar successfully completed a career-long 74 yards for a touchdown in a game against New Orleans on November 17th. He registered an NFL record for most rushing yards by a quarterback in a single game with 173 yards at Minnesota on December 1st.

He then tied for third in the team's history for the lowest interception percentage in a season at 1.90 and continued a streak of consecutive passes without an interception that began at St. Louis on January 6, 2002, in the season-finale of the 2001 season and extended to the first quarter versus Baltimore on November 3, 2002. His streak covered 25 straight quarters and 177 passes without an interception. On January 1, 2003, he led the Atlanta Falcons to an upset victory over the heavily favored Green Bay Packers scoring 27-7 in the NFC playoffs, ending the Packers' undefeated playoff record at Lambeau Field. The Falcons would later lose 20-6 to the Philadelphia Eagles in the NFC divisional playoff game.

## Suffers a Setback

During a pre-season game against the Baltimore Ravens on August 16th, the NFL superstar suffered a setback. He fractured his right fibula and missed the first 11 games of the regular season. In Week-13, he made his season debut in relief of the alternant quarterback in the third quarter at Houston on November 30th, completing 8 of 11 passes for 60 yards recording 16 rushing yards on three carries. He posted his first start of the season against Carolina on December 7th, and amassed the third-highest rushing total by a quarterback in NFL history with 141 yards on 14 carries and one score to lead the Falcons to a come-from-behind 20-14 overtime victory. His 141 yards trailed Tobin Rote's 150 yards on November 18, 1951, with Green Bay and his own NFL record of 173 at Minnesota December 1, 2002; on the NFL's all-time list for quarterbacks. Also, the NFL superstar completed 16 of 33 passes for 179 yards accounting for 320 of the team's 380 total offensive yards. On December 20th, Vick engineered a 30-28 victory at Tampa Bay completing 8 of 15 passes for 119 yards and two touchdowns for a passer rating of 119.2. He closed out the season with a 21-14 victory against Jacksonville on December 28th, where he completed 12 of 22 passes for 180 yards with two touchdowns and one interception. Vick ended the season starting four of five games played; he completed 50 of 100 passes for 585 yards with four touchdowns and three interceptions and rushing 40 times for 255 yards and one touchdown while guiding the Falcons to a 3-1 record in the final four weeks of action.

In 2004, Vick was named to his second Pro Bowl game after starting all 15 games played and completing 181 of 321 passes for 2,313 yards with 14 touchdowns and 12 interceptions while he also posted career-highs with 120 carries for 902 yards along with three rushing touchdowns. The 902 rushing yards with a 7.52 average per carry ranked third and second, respectively, in NFL annals for quarterbacks. Vick received the honor of being named NFC Offensive Player of the Week on two separate occasions during the season. In one for his performances at Denver on October 31, he became the first quarterback to throw for more than 250 yards and rush for over 100 yards in the same game. He led the team to an 11-4 record which was the third-best record for a starting quarterback in the team's history behind Chris Chandler (13-1 in 1998) and Steve Bartkowski (12-4 in 1980). Overall, the Falcons finished the season with an 11-5 record, earning a first-round bye in the NFL playoffs for only the third time in franchise history.

The NFL superstar led Falcons rushed for a playoff record 317 yards. He, himself had rushed 119 of them, setting an NFL playoff record for a quarterback. In addition to all this, he threw two touchdown passes against the Rams in the National Football Conference Divisional Playoffs. However, the Eagles again played the role of heart breaker, beating them in the NFC title game 27-10.

On December 23, 2004, he signed a 10-year contract with the Atlanta Falcons worth $130 million with a 37 million dollar signing bonus, and additional income from many product endorsement arrangements making him the highest paid player in NFL history at that time and one of the highest paid ever in sports. This deal included league records, playoff appearances and lucrative endorsements. His deal surpassed the $98 million contract with the Indianapolis Colts that the top money earner signed in March 2005, which was for seven years and guaranteed $34.5 million in bonuses. The NFL superstar's $130 million potential value tops Philadelphia's top quarterback's 12-year, $115 million deal that runs through 2013.

## Against the Saints

In 2005, the NFL superstar was named to his third Pro Bowl game after starting in all 15 games played and completing 214 yards on 102 carries of 387 passes for 2,412 yards with 15 touchdowns and 13 interceptions. He was in the lead with his 597 rushing 5.9 averages with six scores, leading all NFL quarterbacks. His 5.9 average yards per carry led all NFL rushers with at least 100 carries, while helping three of his team players to have career winning years.

On October 22, 2006, in a game against the Pittsburgh Steelers, the NFL superstar played the first game in which he threw three or more touchdowns. Within three quarters, he had completed four touchdowns. The following week against the Cincinnati Bengals, he threw three more with no interceptions and was honored with the NFC Player of the week award. He had a career high-tying four touchdowns passes against Dallas in Week-15. During the 2006 season, he connected on 204 of 388 passes for 2,474 yards with a career-high of 20 touchdowns. He was third in the league in rushing for ten or more yards with 44.

The NFL superstar was first among quarterbacks in all-time rushing yards per game, at 53.5 yards per game. Only two others had more rushing yards at the quarterback position than he. He holds several NFL quarterback rushing records, including most rushing yards of 173 in one game, most 100 yard rushing games of 7, and most rushing yards in a single season of 1,039. During the 2006 season, the NFL superstar had several incidents occur involving an obscene gesture incident, which ruined his sixth season in the league and lead to his being denied selection to the Pro Bowl; this would have been his third straight and fourth over-all.

## Social Support versus Opposition

Although it is sad to say the NFL superstar had little or no social support for his anti-community characteristics in his personal life endeavor. Case in point, somewhere between his being selected by the Atlanta Falcons in the 2001, NFL Draft and early 2007, he was allegedly involved in several incidents that brought his character into question. In 2007, conflicting statements were made by both his father and mother.

The father said he believed his son might possibly have been involved with dog fighting activities as early as 2001. His father went on to say that his son had been staging dog fights in the garage of the family's home in Newport News and kept fighting dogs in the family's backyard, including injured ones. He in effect, said he knew because, he had nursed dogs back to health. He said the NFL superstar had been urged not to engage in the activity, but he continued. In the father's opinion, "This was Mike's thing. And he knows it". The fact that the NFL superstar's father, who now lives in Atlanta, told the *Atlanta Journal-Constitution* that his son had been involved with dog fighting since around 2001 was actually incriminating to his son's case.

The NFL superstar's mother within days responded in support of her son, stating that: "There was no dog fighting at our home. There were no cages". Although, his mother provided support for her son and gave him the benefit of the doubt. His behavior suggested that his defense mechanisms, caused by past experiences and background issues had caused him to resort to automatic survival in a continuous hostile environment, which was activated as a result of his new lifestyle and environment.

## The Deck was Stacked Against Michael

Although, the NFL superstar was playing against a stacked deck, to a great extent he stacked it against himself. In early 2004, two men were arrested in Virginia for distributing marijuana. The truck they were driving was registered to the NFL superstar. The Falcons' coach recalled that he lectured the superstar at that time on the importance of his reputation, on choosing the right friends, and staying out of trouble for the good of his team and the community.

On October 10, 2004, the NFL superstar and other members of his party were at Atlanta's Hartsfield International Airport to board an AirTran afternoon flight to Newport News, Virginia. While they were passing through a security checkpoint, a security camera caught two members of the party picking up an expensive watch which belonged to a security screener. After watching the theft on a security camera, the security screener filed a police report; however, he did get his watch back from them, six days later.

An Atlanta police inquiry requested the NFL superstar's response, which was declined by his representatives. Then in March 2005, a civil lawsuit was filed against him by a woman alleging she had had an unfavorable contact with the NFL superstar, during autumn 2002. On April 24, 2006, it was revealed that the lawsuit had been settled out of court for an undisclosed figure. On November 26, 2006, after a Falcons' loss to the New Orleans Saints in the Georgia Dome, the NFL superstar held up his two middle fingers making an obscene gesture toward fans after being booed. He was consequently fined $10,000 by the NFL for his obscene gesture, and agreed to donate another $10,000 to charity.

# Chapter Four

## Contrasting the Two Situations

### The Doctor Arrested for Euthanasia

The doctor and two nurses were arrested in the deaths of patients at a New Orleans hospital. They were accused of injecting four patients with lethal doses, cocktail doses of morphine and a sedative known as '*Versed*' during the chaotic situations, which occurred in the days after Hurricane Katrina as flooding overwhelmed the city. The Doctor, a 50-year-old, head and neck surgeon; and Nurses Cheri Landry, 49, and Lori Budo, 43, each faced four second-degree-murder charges. The arrests came amid a broad state inquiry into more than 200 deaths at hospitals and nursing homes after Katrina destroyed much of the city and knocked out power on August 29, 2005.

According to an affidavit filed by an investigator with the Attorney General's office, the doctor and others worked at Memorial Hospital in the days after the storm and had injected at least four patients with lethal doses of morphine and the sedative '*Versed*'. Attorney General, Charles Foti said: of the patients, ages 61, 66, 89 and 90; "They were not receiving these drugs on any routine basis;" and "When you use both of these drugs, it becomes a lethal cocktail which guarantees you're going to die."

The doctor's lawyer said she had continued practicing in Baton Rouge and was arrested in her scrubs as she came home from work. The Doctor's lawyer said of the charge: "We vigorously contest this."

The nurses' lawyers said they expect to be exonerated. The legal team further said: many other involved health care providers were abandoned in a flooded hospital, and they did everything they could to help the sick and needy people, and their efforts were completely heroic. Forty-seven patients died at Memorial; according to the Attorney General's office who did not specify just how many of those deaths were suspect and/or criminal acts. An attorney representing the families of about a dozen people who died at Memorial said: "The truth needs to be told," and "I think the staff thought they were being merciful, but ... no one can play *God*."

I believe the doctor got away with murder because she had legal representation provided by the justice system's discretionary power to discriminate and because she was a member of the dominant status class group. It is these two elements which allow certain individuals to get away with crimes through laws imposed by unjust circumstances; and old rules of law made by men, which are inhumane forms of injustice that serve to punish those who do not fall within these two elements: that of <u>legal representation; and membership within the dominant society.</u>

## Cleared of All Charges

Although the doctor acted in the same way as Jack Kovorkian, who assisted many terminally ill patients to die through euthanasia; on July 24, 2007 an announcement was made that a Louisiana grand jury declined to indict the doctor. The grand jury's refusal to indict the doctor of murdering four seriously ill patients with lethal injections effectively closed the books on the only mercy-killing case during the desperate aftermath of Hurricane Katrina. A fact which was later reported by news sources revealed that no testimonies of medical experts were ever heard by this jury. Days after when another jury acquitted, two nursing-home owners in dozens of Hurricane Katrina related patient deaths a prosecutor said, that no charges would be filed in a similar case involving a nursing home that was run by an order of Roman Catholic nuns. Nineteen elderly residents of Lafon nursing home, run by the Sisters of the Holy Family in New Orleans, died during the days after Katrina hit on August 29, 2005. Flooding destroyed much of the food, drinking water and medicine inside the sweltering building; and it took days for help to arrive.

The doctor admitted giving the injections to the patients, but insisted she did so only to relieve their pain, not to euthanize them as prosecutors had charged. It is reported that she said: "All of us need to remember the magnitude of human suffering that occurred in the city of New Orleans in the wake of Hurricane Katrina, so that we can be sure that this never happens again." She further said: "That no health care professional should ever be falsely accused in a rush to judgment." Attorney General Charles Foti stood by his accusations and said medical experts and reams of evidence had concluded the deaths were homicides, not accidental as the doctor insisted. Attorney General Foti was also reported as saying: "Our investigation, the statement of witnesses, and the opinions of experts provided us with a reasonable belief that crimes had been committed." Foti alleged that the four patients, the doctor medicated would have survived, if she had not injected them with drugs. Many in New Orleans were behind the doctor, and hundreds of them demonstrated this by waving banners in support of her at the City Park.

The president of the Louisiana State Nurses Association said the case threatens to cause medical practitioners to think twice about whether to help people during disasters. Also, she said: "This makes it really hard for people who say okay, we want to work in disasters, but then we're going to be viewed as potential criminals." "It's a very scary thing". In a statement issued regarding the Sisters of the Holy Family by District Attorney Eddie Jordan; he determined that, after a thorough review, no criminal conduct had occurred. Attorney Evans Schmidt, who represents the religious order said: "The sisters are very gratified and relieved." "It has been a long, hard two years." This was the last case, in which workers responsible for caring for patients, who died in Katrina's chaotic aftermath had been investigated for possible criminal wrong doing. No one was convicted in any of these cases. Charges against the two nurses were dropped. New Orleans Parish District Attorney said no other criminal charges would be brought against the doctor. She still faces lawsuits, filed by relatives of the patients, who died however. She told a news conference that she: "Fell to her knees and thanked *God*" when she was told of the decision. In my opinion, it was not *God*, who had saved her, but it was in fact the due process of an injustice formed by a legal system using its discretionary power to discriminate in her favor. The State Attorney General investigated the deaths and turned over the results a year ago without making a recommendation on whether to seek criminal charges. The district attorney's office statement did not refer to the acquittals of the owners of a nursing home in neighboring St. Bernard Parish on charges of negligent homicide and cruelty. His staff said he would have no further comment. This again showed a system gone wrong. Some things are just swept under the carpet so to speak. Where is the value for human life?

State prosecutors alleged that the owners of St. Rita's Nursing Home were criminally responsible for 35 patient deaths, but a jury disagreed. Like St. Rita's owners, the operators at Lafon decided that keeping their frail residents at the home was safer than trying to move them. However, two days before Katrina made landfall, the Sisters of the Holy Family evacuated elderly nuns living on the second floor of the nursing home, but not the lay residents on the first floor. They evacuated 60 nuns who were living in the motherhouse across the street; while 20 staff members, including half a dozen nuns, rode out the hurricane at the nursing home with more than 100 residents. Although flooding was about 3 feet deep on the first floor of the building, the staff was able to evacuate residents to the second floor. Much of the food, drinking water and medicine were destroyed by the flooding. Conditions deteriorated further when the generator failed, causing temperatures inside the home to soar.

Staff members flagged down emergency vehicles to try to get help, but none arrived until the fourth day when a staff member's relative found a bus. Three dozen residents were taken to a nursing home in Houma, Louisiana. The next day, two *Federal Emergency Management Agency* workers arranged for a squadron of Black Hawk helicopters to take the remaining residents to a makeshift hospital at New Orleans' Louis Armstrong International Airport.

Administrators of the Sisters of the Holy Family an *African-American* religious order founded by a free woman of *African* descent in 1842, declined to provide interviews, citing the unresolved criminal investigation and wrongful-death lawsuits filed against them by relatives of victims. The order plans to reopen the nursing home once renovations are completed. Schmidt said: "It's a very important ministry to the sisters," and "Before Katrina it was the oldest continuously operating nursing home in the United States." Several lawsuits are still pending against the sisters, the owners and another Hurricane Katrina case, in which criminal charges had been sought.

## Arrested for Dog fighting

On April 25, 2007, widespread media publicity was drawn by the discovery of evidence of unlawful dog fighting activities at a property owned by the NFL superstar in a rural county in southeast Virginia. After the discovery of extensive facilities used for dog fighting at his 15 acre property near Smithfield, Virginia, he and three other men were arrested on federal felony charges related to their involvement with an illegal interstate dog fighting ring known as Bad Newz Kennels.

The NFL superstar was indicted and eventually pled guilty to federal dog fighting charges, when he was accused of financing the operation. He directly participated in the dog fights and executions, and personally handled thousands of dollars generated through related gambling activities. On December 10, 2007, the NFL superstar was sentenced to 23 months in federal prison, to be followed by three years of supervised probation. A United States District Court Judge in Richmond said: he was "convinced that it was not a momentary lack of judgment" on the superstar part, and that he was a "full-partner" in the dog fighting ring.

Further, the Judge noted that the superstar's lack of cooperation in the earlier stages of the investigation, as well as his continuous lies and his drug use after conviction while free on bond awaiting sentencing. The Judge noted that, despite the superstar's claims that he accepted responsibility for his actions, his failure to cooperate fully with federal officials coupled with a failed drug test and a failed polygraph, showed that he had not accepted full responsibility for funding, promoting and facilitating this cruel and inhumane sporting activity. All four men faced trials on separate state charges after felony indictments were returned by a local grand jury. The superstar's trial in Surry County

Circuit Court was set for April 2, 2008. If convicted on each of the two state felony charges he faced, the maximum penalty, which totaled 10 years in a Virginia penitentiary.

## Federal Criminal Prosecution

In July of 2007, federal authorities charged the NFL superstar and three other men with felony charges for unlawfully operating an interstate dog fighting venture; known as "Bad Newz Kennels" for six-years at Vick's 15-acre property in Surry County, Virginia. He was accused of financing the operation, directly participating in dog fights and executions, and personally handling thousands of dollars in related gambling activities. By August 20th, he and each of the other three co-defendants had agreed to separate plea bargains on the federal charges. They were expected to each receive federal prison sentences of 12 months to a maximum of five years.

On August 24th, the NFL superstar filed his plea documents with the federal court. He pled guilty to one felony count of conspiracy in operating an interstate dog fighting ring. In addition, he admitted to providing most of the financing for the operation as well as participating directly in several dog fights in Virginia, Maryland, North Carolina and South Carolina. He admitted to sharing in the proceeds from these dog fights. He further admitted that he knew his colleagues killed several dogs that did not perform well enough. However, while he admitted to providing most of the money for gambling on the fights, he denied placing any side bets on the dog fights. He further denied actually killing any dogs himself.

On August 27, 2007, U.S. District Judge accepted his guilty plea. In the scheduled December 10, 2007, sentencing the NFL superstar faced a maximum of five years in prison, a fine of $250,000 and three years of supervised probation upon his release. Prosecutors asked to have him sentenced 12-18 months (which is the minimum amount possible under the federal sentencing guidelines) if he cooperated with the government as he had agreed to in the terms of his original plea bargain.

The terms of his plea agreement included a clause, in which he agreed to forfeit his right to appeal any sentence imposed upon him.

Though prosecutors asked for a lower-end sentence for him, the Judge had the authority to increase the sentence up to the maximum limit. The Judge had in fact informed two of the NFL superstar's co-defendants that the brutality of killing the dogs warranted that sentencing exceeds the guidelines in their cases. A significant portion of the plea agreement involved the NFL superstar cooperating with federal authorities in pursuing other dog fighting cases as well as a complete allocation of his role in the Bad Newz Kennels, including detailing his role in the killing of dogs after the fights.

The allocution proved to be a sticking point, as both the federal prosecutors and the Federal Bureau of Investigation agents reported that Vick was giving contradictory statements about how dogs had been killed, what his role in the killings were, how many dogs were killed, and other vital details. According to reporters who spoke to the Judge after the sentencing hearing, the NFL superstar's pre-sentencing behavior, especially during an FBI polygraph administered in October 2007, showed that he was being deceptive. When asked direct questions regarding the killing of the dogs, which was a primary factor in determining the length of his sentence, the NFL superstar answers were questionable.

## The Federal Sentencing

On November 30, 2007, the other two co-defendants were sentenced by the same Judge to 18 to 21 months in federal prison respectively. The punishments each of which were higher than recommended by federal prosecutors included three years of supervised probation following their release from prison. The other one was sentenced later on December 14, 2007, but, unlike the other two he agreed to testify against the NFL superstar at trial before he also accepted a plea agreement. The news media reported that statements from the November 30, 2007, hearing made it clear that this co-defendant; led Bad Newz Kennels. According to arguments presented in United States District Court during the sentencing hearings he guided others who were newcomers to the dog fighting underworld. An attorney argued before the Judge that the third co-defendant was known as "the dog man, an experienced dog fighter and trainer."

Observers speculated that the NFL superstar could be released from prison, as early as latter part of 2009, or as late as 2019. After release from prison, his return to professional football would depend upon the terms of his probation, the possibility of reinstatement by the NFL, his physical condition as well as the possibility of finding a potential team. It is possible that any team, which might consider him at that time would want to look at Vick for other positions. One senior NFL analyst stated: "I am not sure they would bring him back as a quarterback". One magazine reporter said: "It's unlikely that he would be able to play in the Canadian Football League, as it is nearly impossible for a convicted felon to get a Canadian visa". As his last co-defendant was due to be sentenced in federal court on December 14th, observers agreed that the NFL superstar's pending trial in Virginia in April 2008, remained the largest unknown factor for his future.

A United States Federal District Court convicted and sentenced him in 2007, and a 2008 trial was scheduled for related Virginia state felony charges for his role in the dog fighting ring as well as related gambling activities. He is currently being held in the United States Penitentiary at Leavenworth, Kansas for 23 months on charges of running a "cruel and inhumane" dog fighting ring and lying about it.

## Suspension by the NFL

Hours after the NFL superstar pled guilty in the Bad Newz Kennels dog fighting investigation, the NFL suspended Vick indefinitely without pay. In a letter written to him, the Commissioner said: that since the NFL superstar had admitted to conduct that was "not only illegal", but also cruel and reprehensible, that he had barred him from reporting to training camp while the league conducted its own investigation into the matter. Any chance of him playing a down in the NFL in 2007, were all but wiped out at his July 26th, arraignment as the terms of his bail barred him from leaving Virginia for any reason before the trials.

While he is technically a first-time offender under the NFL's Personal Conduct Policy, the commissioner handed down a harsher suspension because the NFL superstar admitted that he provided most of the money for the gambling side of the operation. The NFL does not allow its players to be involved in any form of gambling, and even first-time offenders risk being banned for life. It initially appeared that the commissioner had cleared the way for the Falcons to release the NFL superstar since he ruled that his involvement in gambling activity breached his contract. However, left open the possibility of reinstatement depending on how well he cooperated with state and federal authorities. He is also reported as saying; the team had no immediate plans to cut ties with the NFL superstar, citing salary-cap issues.

On August 27th, he was suspended from his National Football League quarterback position, which he had under contract with the Atlanta Falcons team. Falcons' owner said in a press conference that the Falcons would seek to recover a portion of the NFL superstar signing bonus; within days the Falcons sought to reclaim bonus money paid. On August 29th, the Falcons sent a letter to the NFL superstar demanding that he reimburse them for $20 million of the $37 million bonus. The case was sent to arbitration; the arbitrator agreed with the Falcons' contentions that the NFL superstar knew he was engaging in illegal activity when he signed his new contract in 2004, and that he even used the bonus money to pay for the operations. On October 10th, an arbitrator ruled that he had to reimburse the Falcons for $19.97 million.

With his employment suspended and most product endorsement relationships terminated, three banks filed multi-million dollar civil law suits to recover about $5 million in loans to Vick, that they claimed to be in default of terms. He is now serving a 23 month sentence of incarceration for criminal conspiracy resulting from felonious dog fighting.

## State Criminal Prosecution

Long anticipated separate Virginia charges against all four men were placed following indictments by the Surry County grand jury when it met on September 25th. The principal evidence considered was the sworn statements of the defendants during their plea agreement process before the federal court, although the indictments were for different charges. The NFL superstar is charged with two class six felonies in

Virginia, which carry a maximum penalty of five years imprisonment for conviction on each charge.

He was scheduled to face a jury trial in Surry County Circuit Court on April 2, 2008. He turned himself into authorities in November 2007, to begin serving an anticipated jail sentence on the federal dog fighting conspiracy charge. As of December 4th, he was being held in Northern Neck Regional Jail in Warsaw, Virginia. His co-defendants were also assigned trial dates. They faced a jury trial on March 5, 2008 and were sentenced to 18 months to 21 months for his participation. The confessed "dog man trial" was May 7th. He received the lightest sentence of the four involved in the operations of the dog fighting ring and was released after serving only two (2) months.

## The Pressure too Strong

While free on bail the NFL superstar tested positive for marijuana in a random drug test which was a violation of the conditions of his release imposed while he was awaiting sentencing on his felony conviction. His positive urine sample was submitted on September 13, 2007, according to a document filed in U.S. District Court on September 26th, by a federal probation officer. As a result, the U.S. District Judge ordered him confined to his Hampton, Virginia home between 10 p.m. and 6 a.m. with electronic monitoring until his court hearing date in December. The NFL superstar was also ordered to submit to random drug testing. In November 2007, he turned himself in early, to begin receiving time-served against his likely federal prison sentence. He was initially held at Northern Neck Regional Jail in Warsaw, Virginia, awaiting sentencing on federal convictions on December 10, 2007.

## Disposition of Dogs

As of October 2, 2007, the forty-nine dogs that were seized in April remained in animal shelters in Hampton Roads and central Virginia. An evaluation performed by American Society for the Prevention of Cruelty to Animals showed that one animal, identified as #2621, was aggressive to the point the evaluation could not be completed. The dog also had a history of biting people. The U.S. District Judge ordered that it be euthanized. The U.S. Attorney's Office in Richmond would eventually make an announcement in court filings that the other 48 canines "may be safe enough to place in the community with strict conditions."

On October 16th, the Judge acted on a government motion requesting an animal law expert, a Professor of Law at Valparaiso University School of Law in Indiana, serve as the guardian-special master to oversee the possible placement or euthanasia of the 48 remaining dogs. The Judge also granted a request by the U.S. Attorney's Office, who requested that each of the remaining pit bulls be spayed, if female or neutered if male and that they have a microchip implanted.

In November of 2007, the NFL superstar was observed attempting to liquidating some of his real estate assets, notably the dog-fighting estate near Smithfield, Virginia one of several of his multi-million dollar homes, which are located in Suffolk, Virginia, Atlanta, Georgia, and the South Beach section of Miami. On October 20, 2007 it was reported; that the home near Atlanta was listed for sale at an asking price of $4.5 million. At the request of federal authorities before his sentencing in federal court, the NFL superstar agreed to deposit nearly $1 million dollars into an escrow account to use to reimburse costs of caring for the confiscated dogs, most of whom, are now being offered up for adoption on a selective basis under supervision of a court-appointed specialist. Experts say some of the animals will likely require individual care for the rest of their lives.

## Endorsements and Business Activity

During his NFL career, the superstar became the spokesman for many companies. His endorsement contracts included such powerful brands as EA Sports, Coca-Cola, Powerade, Kraft, Rawlings, Hasbro and Air Tran. His football contract along with his endorsements had him ranked 33 among Forbes' Top 100 Celebrities in 2005. As early as two years later, he was not even mentioned amongst *Forbes* Top 100 Celebrities. Even before the animal cruelty case began to surface in 2007, his corporate status had deteriorated; apparently due to extensive bad press. Among the negative incidents cited by observers was the incident regarding his middle finger gesture made toward Atlanta football fans in 2006. His endorsement deals with at least five companies (Coca-Cola, EA Sports, Kraft Foods, Hasbro and Air Tran) have expired over the past few years and none have been renewed.

## Loses Lucrative Endorsement

On May 8, 2007, AirTran chose not to renew their relationship with the NFL superstar. Although, the Airlines made no public statements regarding their reasons for ending their endorsement relationships; it would appear that it was a result of both his alledged criminal issues and his missed appearance on Capitol Hill on April 24, 2007.

The police search was made at his property near Smithfield, Virginia later that same week. By then the dog fighting investigation had become widely known. Comments made by the NFL superstar's publicist on May 3rd, must have been especially stinging to Air Tran; when he blamed the airline for the quarterback's failure to arrive in Washington to speak before Congress. Air Tran responded by saying the NFL superstar: "had ample opportunities to get to his destination on Air Tran, but chose not to."

## The Impact of Publicity

Following the widespread publicity of the ongoing dog fighting cases and details of the alleged brutality of executing dogs not considered being vicious or aggressive many companies suspended or terminated his endorsements and withdrew Vick-related products from sales. The fact that such notable people as hip-hop mogul, sent a letter to the NFL superstar corporate sponsors condemning dog fighting did not help his souring public image either.

On July 18, 2007, following extensive media coverage concerning the contents of the NFL superstar 18-page federal indictment of the previous day, Neil Schwartz, director of marketing for SportScanInfo, a company which tracks sporting goods sales, told the *Atlanta Journal-Constitution*: "I just think it's going to be really hard for the NFL superstar to somehow repair his public image unless these charges are totally false. American people are incredibly forgiving, but the heinous nature of what went on here may be a whole different ballgame." Also, the same article quoted Bill Sutton, a professor of sports business at the University of Central Florida as saying: "You won't find him anywhere" in advertising or marketing in the near future. MSNBC quoted David Carter, founder of the Sports Business Group, a Southern California-based provider of strategic sports-marketing services as saying, "Number one, animal cruelty is something no one will tolerate. Number two, you have the underbelly of possible gambling. Number three, you have the strength of animal advocacy groups. They aren't going away".

According to the *Virginian-Pilot* in a July 19, 2007 article, the NFL superstar's biggest marketing deal at that time was with *Nike*. Later on the same day, *USA Today* reported that his legal troubles had prompted *Nike* to suspend the release of their latest product line named after him, telling retailers it would not release a "fifth signature shoe, the Air Zoom Vick V, that summer."

On July 27th, *Nike* announced it "has suspended the NFL superstar's contract without pay, and would not sell any more of his products at *Nike* owned retail outlets at this time." However, the company said it had not terminated the contract, as animal-rights activists had urged. That same day, *Adidas* announced that its *Reebok* division would stop selling his football jerseys and the NFL said it had pulled all Vick-related items from NFLShop.com, including Falcons jerseys customized with his name and number. Within days Donruss decided to pull his card from any future 2007 releases, according to Beckett Media, which covers the collectibles industry. Upper Deck, another trading card company took similar action.

On July 31st, St. Louis-based sporting goods manufacturer, which used the NFL superstar likeness to sell merchandise and modeled a football using his name, ended its relationship as well. That same day, Dick's Sporting Goods and Sports Authority stores, part of a major chain stopped selling related goods. Upon the filing of the NFL superstar Plea Agreement and Statement of Facts with the federal court in Richmond, *Nike* announced it had terminated his contract; which had earlier been suspended. On August 29, 2007, an *eBay* auction for 22 Vick football cards, chewed up and slobbered on by two Missouri dogs ended with a final bid of $7,400. All proceeds are expected to be donated to the Humane Society.

In my opinion the NFL superstar was unfairly victimized by the justice system for the crime he committed versus that of many first time offenders. His first criminal offense caused his world to turn againt him. It is a shame, that he was not sentenced to counseling and placed on probation which would have allowed him to continue to make an economic contribution to society. Not one stood with him; although I am sure he had an expectation of some type of support from his world, which benefited so greatly from his contributions to the sports world. *"Justice is supposed to be blind"*, it is not.

## Possible Future with the NFL

The prospects of the NFL superstar returning to professional football were the subject of much conjecture after his suspension. The most serious obstacles were clearly the length of imprisonment and possible impact of probationary restrictions afterward. Assuming he gets time off for good behavior, his earliest release date would be somewhere between May and October 2009, according to his attorneys. That would make his return to play possible as early as the 2009 season assuming all other factors were favorable. Missing two full seasons and the physical regimen could be a serious disruption in a career, but it is not impossible that he could successfully return to play at that point. It is likely however, that teams considering him at that time would want to look at him for other positions. One senior NFL analyst stated: "I am not sure they would bring him back as a quarterback".

The estimated release date is based on the assumption that the state of Virginia does not impose any additional prison time; even after any possible convictions steaming from the two additional felony counts tried against him in Surry Circuit Court in approximately April of 2008. These additional charges could net him a total of 10 years in addition to his federal time. Any additional prison time added by Virginia, of which a maximum of ten years is possible, would lengthen his time away from the NFL which would substantially reduce the likelihood of his successful return; even in a different position than as quarterback. In the most extreme case of a maximum sentence, Vick would be 39 years old by his release date; since Virginia laws have no provisions for parole. Even without considering these factors it is possible that the

NFL superstar's life has been ruined by these unnecessary convictions based on an unspoken discretion to discriminate against status cast group members.

## Conclusion

Each of these two individuals, the Doctor and the NFL superstar are well-known in their professions; however the same old methods of administering justice based on status seems apparent in these particular cases. One of these individuals, the doctor because of her heritage has the dominant society's support for automatic legal representation. The other, the NFL superstar lacks the support of the dominant society because of his heritage, so he must make an asserted effort to gain legal representation. The NFL superstar accepted as many did in his environment a behavior style unacceptable to the mainstream culture, but consistant with his mainstream. Dog fighting was an acceptable past-time in his community and a part of his natural environment, so he therefore without realizing the full consequence of his actions, he continued within his natural comfort zone; however he did not grasp the legal ramifications.

The problem is that two people from two different cultures and status-cast groups of society both committed crimes against society. However, the presiding Judges in two separate jurisdictions found the Doctor a woman raised upper-middle class; not guilty of inhumane treatment towards human beings that she actually killed. While, the presiding Judge in another jurisdiction found the NFL superstar a young man raised in the projects of Newport News, Virginia guilty of all charges and sentenced him by throwing the book at him and imprisoning him for inhumane treatment towards dogs. This, in spite of the fact that his economic contribution to society was greater and his crimes of killing dogs should have carried a lesser value. It appears society in their support of a justice system using its implied legal discretionary right to discriminate failed to apply *Blind Justice*; and is willing to bid against their own economic interest to support a discriminatory justice for a high profile wealthy young man belonging to a low status-cast group. Without both of these elements, due process of law will fail an individual on each and every occasion because they both work hand-in-hand (legal representation and support by the dominant society).


*Carrie Johnson*
Editor/Coordinator

*Arthur Stovall, Ph.D.*
Story Analyst

# About the Author

Reverend Pou refers to himself as a country boy straight from the Mississippi bottoms. He was born on October 31, 1950, in a small town in Mississippi by the name of Waynesboro. During his first three years of school he attended school in a real schoolhouse which served as both the town's church and school. After leaving that school, he went on to attend a school in downtown Waynesboro by the name of Riverview High, where he was an active student. He was on the basketball team and played a musical instrument (the Tuba) in the band. According to Reverend Pou it was the best high school band in Mississippi. One of the reasons, he believed the band was so great, he thought was the jazzy music played; he said: "the band won all their competitions". It was said: "Jackson State has never seen a band that could sight read music the way this band did".

Reverend Pou remembers a time during one of his basketball games that he retrieved a rebound ball, and the official called a foul on him. He had moved so rapidly during the rebound that he failed to observe the position in which he had landed, on one of the other player! The official said to him, look under your knees; his knees were in the other team's player's back. He said: "I was motivated to rebound the basketball, because I enjoyed the girls screaming when I jumped for the basketball". Reverend Pou graduated from high school in 1967 and went on to obtain a Bachelor of Science degree in Human Services and Management from the University of Phoenix.

Reverend Willie Pou eventually moved to Las Vegas, Nevada, where he has resided since May 20, 1970. He is active in both his church and community. He sings in three different choirs; two of them at Second Baptist Church of Las Vegas where he is a member. The other is a community choir known as GMWA Silver State Choir. Also, Reverend Pou preaches at St. Mark Missionary Baptist Church. Before coming to Las Vegas, he was engaged to two beautiful ladies at the same time, a Creole lady from New Orleans, Louisiana, and another from Sandusky, Ohio. He traveled to Las Vegas by way of Ohio. He has affectionate memories of Ohio and his employment at Cedar Point theme park on the shore of Lake Erie just about an hour west of Cleveland. The theme park as he remembers had the largest roller coaster in the world. There were always two places he dreamed of spending the rest of his life, Las Vegas or New Orleans. He chose to live in Las Vegas where he now enjoys the lifestyle it offers.